50 Delicious Lime Recipes for Home

By: Kelly Johnson

Table of Contents

- Key Lime Pie
- Lime Cilantro Chicken
- Lime and Coconut Muffins
- Lime Sorbet
- Lime Margarita
- Lime and Avocado Salsa
- Lime Ginger Chicken
- Thai Lime and Chili Noodles
- Lime Cheesecake
- Lime and Mint Iced Tea
- Lime-Coconut Rice
- Lime-Cilantro Rice
- Lime and Honey Glazed Salmon
- Lime-Pickle Chicken Wings
- Lime Shortbread Cookies
- Lime-Mint Mojito
- Lime-Tarragon Chicken Salad
- Lime and Basil Pesto
- Lime Shrimp Tacos
- Lime and Chia Seed Pudding
- Lime-Roasted Vegetables
- Lime-Coconut Cake
- Lime-Coconut Energy Balls
- Lime and Cucumber Gazpacho
- Lime and Spicy Black Beans
- Lime-Cilantro Quinoa
- Lime and Garlic Grilled Shrimp
- Lime-Lemonade
- Lime and Berry Smoothie
- Lime and White Chocolate Cheesecake
- Lime and Pineapple Salsa
- Lime-Honey Dressing
- Lime-Infused Chicken Wings
- Lime and Cilantro Beef Tacos

- Lime and Jalapeño Marinade
- Lime and Coconut Chicken Curry
- Lime-Pineapple Sorbet
- Lime-Ginger Dressing
- Lime and Cilantro Soup
- Lime and Banana Bread
- Lime-Peppercorn Pork Chops
- Lime-Lavender Muffins
- Lime and Chipotle Salsa
- Lime-Mango Chutney
- Lime and Coconut Smoothie
- Lime-Glazed Donuts
- Lime and Blackberry Crumble
- Lime-Coconut Energy Bars
- Lime and Tequila Chicken
- Lime and Cilantro Cornbread

Key Lime Pie

Ingredients:

- **For the Crust:**
    - 1 ½ cups graham cracker crumbs
    - ¼ cup granulated sugar
    - 6 tbsp unsalted butter, melted
- **For the Filling:**
    - 1 cup key lime juice (fresh or bottled)
    - 1 can (14 oz) sweetened condensed milk
    - 4 large egg yolks
    - 1 tsp vanilla extract
- **For the Topping:**
    - Whipped cream
    - Lime zest for garnish

Instructions:

1. **Prepare the Crust:**
    1. Preheat your oven to 350°F (175°C).
    2. In a medium bowl, combine the graham cracker crumbs, granulated sugar, and melted butter. Mix until the crumbs are evenly coated.
    3. Press the mixture into the bottom and up the sides of a 9-inch pie dish.
    4. Bake for 8-10 minutes, then let it cool completely.
2. **Prepare the Filling:**
    1. In a large bowl, whisk together the key lime juice, sweetened condensed milk, egg yolks, and vanilla extract until smooth.
    2. Pour the filling into the cooled crust.
3. **Bake the Pie:**
    1. Bake in the preheated oven for 15-18 minutes, or until the filling is set and slightly firm around the edges.
    2. Turn off the oven and let the pie cool inside with the door slightly ajar for 1 hour.
    3. Refrigerate for at least 4 hours, or overnight, to chill and set.
4. **Serve:**
    1. Top with whipped cream and garnish with lime zest before serving.

Lime Cilantro Chicken

Ingredients:

- 4 boneless, skinless chicken breasts
- ¼ cup lime juice
- 2 tbsp olive oil
- 2 cloves garlic, minced
- 1 tsp ground cumin
- 1 tsp paprika
- ½ tsp chili powder
- 1 tsp salt
- ¼ tsp black pepper
- ¼ cup fresh cilantro, chopped

Instructions:

1. **Marinate the Chicken:**
    1. In a bowl, combine lime juice, olive oil, garlic, cumin, paprika, chili powder, salt, and pepper.
    2. Place the chicken breasts in a resealable plastic bag or shallow dish and pour the marinade over them.
    3. Seal the bag or cover the dish and refrigerate for at least 30 minutes, or up to 4 hours for more flavor.
2. **Cook the Chicken:**
    1. Preheat your grill or stovetop grill pan to medium-high heat.
    2. Remove the chicken from the marinade and discard the marinade.
    3. Grill the chicken for 6-7 minutes per side, or until fully cooked and the internal temperature reaches 165°F (74°C).
    4. Remove from heat and let it rest for a few minutes.
3. **Garnish and Serve:**
    1. Sprinkle the chicken with fresh cilantro before serving.

Lime and Coconut Muffins

Ingredients:

- 1 ¾ cups all-purpose flour
- ¾ cup granulated sugar
- ½ cup shredded coconut
- 1 tbsp baking powder
- ¼ tsp salt
- ¼ cup unsalted butter, melted
- ½ cup coconut milk
- 2 large eggs
- 2 tbsp lime juice
- Zest of 1 lime

Instructions:

1. **Prepare the Muffin Batter:**
    1. Preheat your oven to 350°F (175°C) and line a muffin tin with paper liners.
    2. In a large bowl, whisk together the flour, sugar, shredded coconut, baking powder, and salt.
    3. In another bowl, whisk together the melted butter, coconut milk, eggs, lime juice, and lime zest.
    4. Pour the wet ingredients into the dry ingredients and stir until just combined. Do not overmix.
2. **Bake the Muffins:**
    1. Divide the batter evenly among the muffin cups.
    2. Bake for 18-20 minutes, or until a toothpick inserted into the center of a muffin comes out clean.
    3. Allow the muffins to cool in the tin for 5 minutes before transferring them to a wire rack to cool completely.

Lime Sorbet

Ingredients:

- 1 cup lime juice (freshly squeezed)
- 1 cup granulated sugar
- 1 cup water
- Zest of 2 limes
- Optional: mint leaves for garnish

Instructions:

1. **Prepare the Syrup:**
    1. In a medium saucepan, combine the water and sugar. Heat over medium heat, stirring until the sugar is fully dissolved.
    2. Remove from heat and let it cool to room temperature.
2. **Combine and Freeze:**
    1. Stir the lime juice and lime zest into the cooled syrup.
    2. Pour the mixture into an ice cream maker and churn according to the manufacturer's instructions until it reaches a soft-serve consistency.
    3. Transfer the sorbet to a lidded container and freeze for at least 2 hours, or until firm.
3. **Serve:**
    1. Scoop into bowls and garnish with mint leaves if desired.

Lime Margarita

Ingredients:

- 2 oz tequila
- 1 oz lime juice (freshly squeezed)
- 1 oz triple sec
- ½ oz simple syrup (optional, for added sweetness)
- Salt for rimming the glass
- Ice
- Lime wedges for garnish

Instructions:

1. **Prepare the Glass:**
    1. Rub the rim of a margarita glass with a lime wedge.
    2. Dip the rim into a plate of salt to coat.
2. **Mix the Margarita:**
    1. In a shaker, combine the tequila, lime juice, triple sec, and simple syrup (if using).
    2. Fill the shaker with ice and shake vigorously until well chilled.
3. **Serve:**
    1. Strain the mixture into the prepared glass filled with ice.
    2. Garnish with a lime wedge.

Lime and Avocado Salsa

Ingredients:

- 2 ripe avocados, diced
- 1 cup cherry tomatoes, halved
- ¼ cup red onion, finely chopped
- ¼ cup fresh cilantro, chopped
- 1 jalapeño, seeded and finely chopped (optional for heat)
- 2 tbsp lime juice
- Salt and pepper to taste

Instructions:

1. **Combine Ingredients:**
    1. In a medium bowl, gently mix together the diced avocados, cherry tomatoes, red onion, cilantro, and jalapeño (if using).
2. **Season and Serve:**
    1. Drizzle with lime juice and season with salt and pepper.
    2. Stir gently to combine.
    3. Serve immediately with tortilla chips or as a topping for grilled meats.

Lime Ginger Chicken

Ingredients:

- 4 boneless, skinless chicken breasts
- ¼ cup lime juice
- 2 tbsp soy sauce
- 2 tbsp honey
- 2 tbsp vegetable oil
- 1 tbsp fresh ginger, grated
- 2 cloves garlic, minced
- 1 tsp ground cumin
- ½ tsp salt
- ¼ tsp black pepper
- 2 green onions, sliced (for garnish)
- Fresh cilantro, chopped (for garnish)

Instructions:

1. **Prepare the Marinade:**
    1. In a bowl, whisk together lime juice, soy sauce, honey, vegetable oil, grated ginger, minced garlic, cumin, salt, and pepper.
2. **Marinate the Chicken:**
    1. Place the chicken breasts in a resealable plastic bag or shallow dish.
    2. Pour the marinade over the chicken, ensuring it is well coated.
    3. Seal the bag or cover the dish and refrigerate for at least 30 minutes, or up to 4 hours for deeper flavor.
3. **Cook the Chicken:**
    1. Preheat your grill or stovetop grill pan to medium-high heat.
    2. Remove the chicken from the marinade and discard the marinade.
    3. Grill the chicken for 6-7 minutes per side, or until fully cooked and the internal temperature reaches 165°F (74°C).
    4. Let the chicken rest for a few minutes before slicing.
4. **Garnish and Serve:**
    1. Garnish with sliced green onions and chopped cilantro before serving.

Thai Lime and Chili Noodles

Ingredients:

- 8 oz rice noodles
- 2 tbsp vegetable oil
- 2 cloves garlic, minced
- 1 red bell pepper, sliced
- 1 cup snap peas
- ¼ cup lime juice
- 2 tbsp fish sauce
- 1 tbsp soy sauce
- 1 tbsp brown sugar
- 1-2 tsp red chili flakes (adjust to taste)
- ¼ cup fresh basil, chopped
- ¼ cup roasted peanuts, chopped (for garnish)

Instructions:

1. **Cook the Noodles:**
    1. Cook the rice noodles according to the package instructions. Drain and set aside.
2. **Prepare the Sauce:**
    1. In a small bowl, whisk together lime juice, fish sauce, soy sauce, brown sugar, and red chili flakes. Set aside.
3. **Stir-Fry the Vegetables:**
    1. Heat vegetable oil in a large skillet or wok over medium-high heat.
    2. Add garlic and cook for 30 seconds until fragrant.
    3. Add red bell pepper and snap peas. Stir-fry for 3-4 minutes, or until vegetables are tender-crisp.
4. **Combine and Serve:**
    1. Add the cooked noodles and sauce to the skillet. Toss everything together until well combined and heated through.
    2. Remove from heat and stir in fresh basil.
    3. Serve garnished with chopped peanuts.

Lime Cheesecake

Ingredients:

- **For the Crust:**
  - 1 ½ cups graham cracker crumbs
  - ¼ cup granulated sugar
  - 6 tbsp unsalted butter, melted
- **For the Filling:**
  - 16 oz cream cheese, softened
  - 1 cup granulated sugar
  - 3 large eggs
  - 1 cup sour cream
  - ½ cup lime juice (freshly squeezed)
  - Zest of 2 limes
  - 1 tsp vanilla extract
- **For the Topping:**
  - Whipped cream
  - Lime zest or lime slices for garnish

Instructions:

1. **Prepare the Crust:**
   1. Preheat your oven to 350°F (175°C).
   2. In a medium bowl, combine graham cracker crumbs, granulated sugar, and melted butter.
   3. Press the mixture into the bottom and up the sides of a 9-inch springform pan.
   4. Bake for 8-10 minutes, then let it cool.
2. **Prepare the Filling:**
   1. In a large bowl, beat the cream cheese until smooth.
   2. Gradually add the sugar and continue to beat until fully combined.
   3. Add the eggs one at a time, mixing well after each addition.
   4. Mix in the sour cream, lime juice, lime zest, and vanilla extract until smooth.
3. **Bake the Cheesecake:**
   1. Pour the filling into the cooled crust.

2. Bake in the preheated oven for 50-60 minutes, or until the center is set and the edges are slightly golden.
3. Turn off the oven and let the cheesecake cool with the door slightly ajar for 1 hour.
4. Refrigerate for at least 4 hours, or overnight, to set.

4. **Serve:**
    1. Top with whipped cream and garnish with lime zest or slices before serving.

Lime and Mint Iced Tea

Ingredients:

- 4 cups water
- 4 black tea bags
- ¼ cup granulated sugar (adjust to taste)
- ¼ cup lime juice (freshly squeezed)
- ¼ cup fresh mint leaves
- Lime slices and mint sprigs for garnish

Instructions:

1. **Brew the Tea:**
    1. Bring 4 cups of water to a boil. Remove from heat and add the tea bags.
    2. Steep for 5 minutes, then remove the tea bags.
2. **Sweeten and Chill:**
    1. Stir in the sugar until fully dissolved.
    2. Add the lime juice and mint leaves.
    3. Let the tea cool to room temperature, then refrigerate until chilled.
3. **Serve:**
    1. Pour over ice and garnish with lime slices and mint sprigs.

Lime-Coconut Rice

Ingredients:

- 1 cup jasmine or basmati rice
- 1 cup coconut milk
- 1 cup water
- 1 tbsp lime juice
- 1 tsp lime zest
- ½ tsp salt
- 1 tbsp chopped fresh cilantro (optional)

Instructions:

1. **Cook the Rice:**
    1. Rinse the rice under cold water until the water runs clear.
    2. In a medium saucepan, combine the coconut milk, water, lime juice, lime zest, and salt. Bring to a boil.
2. **Simmer the Rice:**
    1. Add the rice, reduce the heat to low, and cover.
    2. Simmer for 15-20 minutes, or until the rice is tender and the liquid is absorbed.
3. **Fluff and Serve:**
    1. Fluff the rice with a fork and stir in chopped cilantro if desired.
    2. Serve as a side dish with your favorite main course.

Lime-Cilantro Rice

Ingredients:

- 1 cup jasmine or basmati rice
- 2 cups water
- 1 tbsp lime juice
- 1 tsp lime zest
- 2 tbsp fresh cilantro, chopped
- ½ tsp salt

Instructions:

1. **Cook the Rice:**
   1. Rinse the rice under cold water until the water runs clear.
   2. In a medium saucepan, combine the water, lime juice, lime zest, and salt. Bring to a boil.
2. **Simmer the Rice:**
   1. Add the rice, reduce the heat to low, and cover.
   2. Simmer for 15-20 minutes, or until the rice is tender and the liquid is absorbed.
3. **Fluff and Serve:**
   1. Fluff the rice with a fork and stir in the chopped cilantro.
   2. Serve as a flavorful side dish with your favorite main course.

Lime and Honey Glazed Salmon

Ingredients:

- 4 salmon fillets
- ¼ cup honey
- ¼ cup lime juice (freshly squeezed)
- 2 tbsp soy sauce
- 2 cloves garlic, minced
- 1 tbsp fresh ginger, grated
- 1 tbsp olive oil
- Salt and pepper to taste
- Lime wedges and fresh cilantro for garnish

Instructions:

1. **Prepare the Glaze:**
    1. In a small bowl, whisk together honey, lime juice, soy sauce, minced garlic, and grated ginger.
2. **Marinate the Salmon:**
    1. Season the salmon fillets with salt and pepper.
    2. Brush the glaze generously over the salmon fillets. Let them marinate for at least 15 minutes.
3. **Cook the Salmon:**
    1. Preheat your grill or oven to medium-high heat (375°F or 190°C).
    2. If grilling, lightly oil the grill grates. Place the salmon on the grill and cook for 4-5 minutes per side, or until the salmon flakes easily with a fork. If baking, place the salmon on a baking sheet and bake for 12-15 minutes.
4. **Serve:**
    1. Garnish with lime wedges and fresh cilantro before serving.

Lime-Pickle Chicken Wings

Ingredients:

- 2 lbs chicken wings
- ½ cup lime pickle (store-bought or homemade)
- 2 tbsp vegetable oil
- 1 tbsp lime juice
- 1 tsp cumin
- 1 tsp paprika
- ½ tsp ground turmeric
- ¼ tsp black pepper
- Fresh cilantro for garnish

Instructions:

1. **Marinate the Wings:**
   1. In a large bowl, mix together the lime pickle, vegetable oil, lime juice, cumin, paprika, turmeric, and black pepper.
   2. Add the chicken wings and toss to coat thoroughly.
   3. Cover and refrigerate for at least 1 hour, or overnight for best results.
2. **Cook the Wings:**
   1. Preheat your oven to 400°F (200°C) or prepare your grill for medium-high heat.
   2. Arrange the marinated wings on a baking sheet lined with parchment paper or a grill rack.
   3. Bake in the preheated oven for 35-40 minutes, turning once halfway through, or grill for 20-25 minutes, turning occasionally, until the wings are crispy and cooked through.
3. **Serve:**
   1. Garnish with fresh cilantro before serving.

Lime Shortbread Cookies

Ingredients:

- 1 cup unsalted butter, softened
- ½ cup granulated sugar
- 2 cups all-purpose flour
- 1 tbsp lime zest
- 2 tbsp lime juice
- ¼ tsp salt
- Optional: powdered sugar for dusting

Instructions:

1. **Prepare the Dough:**
    1. Preheat your oven to 325°F (165°C) and line a baking sheet with parchment paper.
    2. In a large bowl, beat the softened butter and granulated sugar together until creamy.
    3. Mix in the lime zest and lime juice.
    4. Gradually add the flour and salt, mixing until just combined.
2. **Shape and Bake:**
    1. Roll the dough out on a floured surface to about ¼ inch thickness.
    2. Cut into desired shapes using cookie cutters.
    3. Place the cookies on the prepared baking sheet and bake for 12-15 minutes, or until the edges are lightly golden.
3. **Cool and Serve:**
    1. Allow cookies to cool completely on a wire rack.
    2. Dust with powdered sugar if desired before serving.

Lime-Mint Mojito

Ingredients:

- 10 fresh mint leaves
- 1 lime, cut into wedges
- 2 tbsp granulated sugar
- 2 oz white rum
- 1 cup ice
- Club soda
- Lime slices and mint sprigs for garnish

Instructions:

1. **Muddle Ingredients:**
    1. In a glass, muddle the mint leaves with the lime wedges and sugar to release the lime juice and mint oils.
2. **Mix the Drink:**
    1. Add the white rum and ice to the glass.
    2. Top with club soda and stir gently to combine.
3. **Serve:**
    1. Garnish with lime slices and mint sprigs before serving.

Lime-Tarragon Chicken Salad

Ingredients:

- 2 cups cooked chicken, shredded or diced
- ¼ cup mayonnaise
- ¼ cup Greek yogurt
- 2 tbsp lime juice
- 1 tbsp fresh tarragon, chopped (or 1 tsp dried tarragon)
- 1 celery stalk, diced
- ¼ cup red onion, finely chopped
- Salt and pepper to taste

Instructions:

1. **Prepare the Dressing:**
    1. In a large bowl, combine mayonnaise, Greek yogurt, lime juice, and chopped tarragon.
2. **Combine the Salad:**
    1. Add the cooked chicken, diced celery, and red onion to the bowl.
    2. Mix until everything is well coated with the dressing.
    3. Season with salt and pepper to taste.
3. **Serve:**
    1. Chill in the refrigerator for at least 30 minutes before serving.
    2. Serve on a bed of greens, in a sandwich, or with crackers.

Lime and Basil Pesto

Ingredients:

- 2 cups fresh basil leaves
- ¼ cup pine nuts (or walnuts)
- ¼ cup grated Parmesan cheese
- 2 cloves garlic
- ¼ cup lime juice
- ½ cup olive oil
- Salt and pepper to taste

Instructions:

1. **Prepare the Pesto:**
   1. In a food processor, combine basil leaves, pine nuts, Parmesan cheese, garlic, and lime juice.
   2. Pulse until finely chopped.
2. **Blend and Season:**
   1. With the food processor running, slowly add the olive oil until the pesto reaches your desired consistency.
   2. Season with salt and pepper to taste.
3. **Serve:**
   1. Use the pesto as a sauce for pasta, a spread for sandwiches, or a topping for grilled meats or vegetables. Store any leftovers in an airtight container in the refrigerator for up to a week.

Lime Shrimp Tacos

Ingredients:

- 1 lb shrimp, peeled and deveined
- 2 tbsp olive oil
- 2 tbsp lime juice (freshly squeezed)
- 2 cloves garlic, minced
- 1 tsp chili powder
- 1 tsp ground cumin
- ½ tsp paprika
- ¼ tsp cayenne pepper (optional)
- Salt and pepper to taste
- 8 small tortillas
- 1 cup shredded cabbage
- ½ cup fresh cilantro, chopped
- Lime wedges for serving
- Salsa or avocado for topping (optional)

Instructions:

1. **Marinate the Shrimp:**
    1. In a bowl, combine olive oil, lime juice, garlic, chili powder, cumin, paprika, cayenne pepper, salt, and pepper.
    2. Add the shrimp and toss to coat. Marinate for 15-20 minutes.
2. **Cook the Shrimp:**
    1. Heat a large skillet over medium-high heat.
    2. Add the marinated shrimp and cook for 2-3 minutes per side, or until pink and opaque.
3. **Assemble the Tacos:**
    1. Warm the tortillas in a dry skillet or microwave.
    2. Fill each tortilla with shredded cabbage and cooked shrimp.
    3. Garnish with chopped cilantro and serve with lime wedges and salsa or avocado if desired.

Lime and Chia Seed Pudding

Ingredients:

- ½ cup chia seeds
- 2 cups coconut milk
- ¼ cup maple syrup or honey
- ¼ cup lime juice (freshly squeezed)
- Zest of 1 lime
- Fresh fruit or berries for topping (optional)

Instructions:

1. **Combine Ingredients:**
    1. In a large bowl, whisk together chia seeds, coconut milk, maple syrup (or honey), lime juice, and lime zest.
2. **Refrigerate:**
    1. Cover the bowl and refrigerate for at least 4 hours, or overnight, to allow the chia seeds to absorb the liquid and thicken.
3. **Serve:**
    1. Stir the pudding before serving and top with fresh fruit or berries if desired.

Lime-Roasted Vegetables

Ingredients:

- 4 cups mixed vegetables (e.g., bell peppers, zucchini, carrots, red onions), cut into bite-sized pieces
- 3 tbsp olive oil
- 2 tbsp lime juice (freshly squeezed)
- 1 tsp ground cumin
- 1 tsp paprika
- 1 tsp dried oregano
- ½ tsp salt
- ¼ tsp black pepper
- Fresh cilantro for garnish (optional)

Instructions:

1. **Prepare the Vegetables:**
    1. Preheat your oven to 400°F (200°C).
    2. In a large bowl, toss the vegetables with olive oil, lime juice, cumin, paprika, oregano, salt, and pepper.
2. **Roast the Vegetables:**
    1. Spread the vegetables in a single layer on a baking sheet.
    2. Roast in the preheated oven for 25-30 minutes, or until tender and lightly browned, stirring halfway through.
3. **Serve:**
    1. Garnish with fresh cilantro if desired and serve warm.

Lime-Coconut Cake

Ingredients:

- **For the Cake:**
    - 1 ¾ cups all-purpose flour
    - 1 cup granulated sugar
    - 1 cup shredded coconut
    - ½ cup unsalted butter, softened
    - ½ cup coconut milk
    - ¼ cup lime juice (freshly squeezed)
    - 2 large eggs
    - 1 ½ tsp baking powder
    - ¼ tsp salt
- **For the Glaze:**
    - 1 cup powdered sugar
    - 2-3 tbsp lime juice (freshly squeezed)
    - 2 tbsp shredded coconut (for garnish)

Instructions:

1. **Prepare the Cake:**
    1. Preheat your oven to 350°F (175°C) and grease a 9-inch round cake pan.
    2. In a bowl, whisk together flour, sugar, shredded coconut, baking powder, and salt.
    3. In another bowl, beat the butter until creamy. Mix in the coconut milk, lime juice, and eggs until well combined.
    4. Gradually add the dry ingredients to the wet ingredients, mixing until just combined.
    5. Pour the batter into the prepared cake pan and smooth the top.
2. **Bake the Cake:**
    1. Bake for 25-30 minutes, or until a toothpick inserted into the center comes out clean.
    2. Allow the cake to cool in the pan for 10 minutes before transferring to a wire rack to cool completely.
3. **Prepare the Glaze:**
    1. In a small bowl, whisk together powdered sugar and lime juice until smooth.

2. Drizzle the glaze over the cooled cake and garnish with shredded coconut.

Lime-Coconut Energy Balls

Ingredients:

- 1 cup dates, pitted
- 1 cup shredded coconut
- ½ cup almonds (or other nuts)
- ¼ cup lime juice (freshly squeezed)
- Zest of 1 lime
- 1 tbsp honey or maple syrup (optional)

Instructions:

1. **Blend the Ingredients:**
    1. In a food processor, combine dates, shredded coconut, almonds, lime juice, and lime zest.
    2. Process until the mixture forms a sticky dough. If the mixture is too dry, add honey or maple syrup.
2. **Form the Balls:**
    1. Roll the mixture into 1-inch balls and place them on a baking sheet lined with parchment paper.
3. **Chill and Serve:**
    1. Refrigerate the energy balls for at least 30 minutes to firm up before serving.

Lime and Cucumber Gazpacho

Ingredients:

- 2 cups cucumber, peeled and chopped
- 1 cup tomatoes, chopped
- ½ cup red bell pepper, chopped
- ¼ cup red onion, chopped
- 2 cloves garlic, minced
- 3 tbsp lime juice (freshly squeezed)
- ¼ cup fresh cilantro, chopped
- 1 tbsp olive oil
- Salt and pepper to taste

Instructions:

1. **Blend the Ingredients:**
    1. In a blender or food processor, combine cucumber, tomatoes, red bell pepper, red onion, garlic, lime juice, and olive oil.
    2. Blend until smooth. Season with salt and pepper to taste.
2. **Chill and Serve:**
    1. Refrigerate the gazpacho for at least 1 hour to chill.
    2. Garnish with fresh cilantro before serving.

Lime and Spicy Black Beans

Ingredients:

- 2 cans (15 oz each) black beans, drained and rinsed
- 2 tbsp olive oil
- 1 onion, chopped
- 2 cloves garlic, minced
- 1 jalapeño, seeded and minced (adjust to taste)
- 1 tsp ground cumin
- ½ tsp smoked paprika
- ½ tsp chili powder
- ¼ cup lime juice (freshly squeezed)
- Salt and pepper to taste
- Fresh cilantro for garnish (optional)

Instructions:

1. **Sauté the Aromatics:**
    1. In a large skillet, heat olive oil over medium heat.
    2. Add onion and cook until translucent, about 5 minutes.
    3. Add garlic and jalapeño, and cook for another 1-2 minutes.
2. **Cook the Beans:**
    1. Stir in cumin, smoked paprika, and chili powder. Cook for 1 minute until fragrant.
    2. Add the black beans and cook for 5-7 minutes, stirring occasionally, until heated through.
    3. Stir in lime juice and season with salt and pepper to taste.
3. **Serve:**
    1. Garnish with fresh cilantro if desired and serve warm.

Lime-Cilantro Quinoa

Ingredients:

- 1 cup quinoa
- 2 cups water or vegetable broth
- 2 tbsp lime juice (freshly squeezed)
- 1 tbsp olive oil
- ¼ cup fresh cilantro, chopped
- ½ tsp ground cumin
- ½ tsp salt
- ¼ tsp black pepper

Instructions:

1. **Cook the Quinoa:**
    1. Rinse quinoa under cold water until the water runs clear.
    2. In a medium saucepan, bring water or vegetable broth to a boil. Add quinoa, reduce heat to low, cover, and simmer for 15 minutes, or until quinoa is tender and liquid is absorbed.
    3. Remove from heat and let it sit, covered, for 5 minutes. Fluff with a fork.
2. **Season and Serve:**
    1. Stir in lime juice, olive oil, chopped cilantro, ground cumin, salt, and pepper.
    2. Serve warm as a side dish or base for salads.

Lime and Garlic Grilled Shrimp

Ingredients:

- 1 lb shrimp, peeled and deveined
- 3 tbsp olive oil
- 2 tbsp lime juice (freshly squeezed)
- 4 cloves garlic, minced
- 1 tsp smoked paprika
- ½ tsp ground cumin
- ¼ tsp cayenne pepper (optional)
- Salt and pepper to taste
- Lime wedges and fresh cilantro for garnish

Instructions:

1. **Marinate the Shrimp:**
    1. In a bowl, combine olive oil, lime juice, minced garlic, smoked paprika, ground cumin, cayenne pepper (if using), salt, and pepper.
    2. Add the shrimp and toss to coat. Marinate for 15-20 minutes.
2. **Grill the Shrimp:**
    1. Preheat your grill to medium-high heat.
    2. Thread the shrimp onto skewers if desired.
    3. Grill for 2-3 minutes per side, or until shrimp are pink and opaque.
3. **Serve:**
    1. Garnish with lime wedges and fresh cilantro before serving.

Lime-Lemonade

Ingredients:

- 1 cup fresh lime juice
- 1 cup fresh lemon juice
- 1 cup granulated sugar (or to taste)
- 4 cups cold water
- Ice
- Lime and lemon slices for garnish

Instructions:

1. **Make the Lemonade:**
    1. In a large pitcher, combine lime juice, lemon juice, and sugar. Stir until the sugar is completely dissolved.
    2. Add cold water and stir well.
2. **Serve:**
    1. Fill glasses with ice and pour lemonade over.
    2. Garnish with lime and lemon slices if desired.

Lime and Berry Smoothie

Ingredients:

- 1 cup mixed berries (fresh or frozen)
- 1 banana
- 1 cup Greek yogurt
- ¼ cup lime juice (freshly squeezed)
- 1 tbsp honey or maple syrup (optional)
- 1 cup ice

Instructions:

1. **Blend the Smoothie:**
    1. In a blender, combine mixed berries, banana, Greek yogurt, lime juice, honey (if using), and ice.
    2. Blend until smooth and creamy.
2. **Serve:**
    1. Pour into glasses and serve immediately.

Lime and White Chocolate Cheesecake

Ingredients:

- **For the Crust:**
    - 1 ½ cups graham cracker crumbs
    - ¼ cup granulated sugar
    - 6 tbsp unsalted butter, melted
- **For the Filling:**
    - 16 oz cream cheese, softened
    - 1 cup granulated sugar
    - 3 large eggs
    - 1 cup sour cream
    - ½ cup white chocolate chips, melted
    - ¼ cup lime juice (freshly squeezed)
    - Zest of 2 limes
    - 1 tsp vanilla extract
- **For the Topping:**
    - Whipped cream
    - Lime zest or white chocolate shavings for garnish

Instructions:

1. **Prepare the Crust:**
    1. Preheat your oven to 325°F (165°C).
    2. In a medium bowl, mix graham cracker crumbs, granulated sugar, and melted butter.
    3. Press mixture into the bottom of a 9-inch springform pan.
    4. Bake for 8-10 minutes and let cool.
2. **Prepare the Filling:**
    1. In a large bowl, beat the cream cheese until smooth.
    2. Gradually add sugar and beat until combined.
    3. Mix in the eggs one at a time.
    4. Add sour cream, melted white chocolate, lime juice, lime zest, and vanilla extract. Mix until smooth.
3. **Bake the Cheesecake:**
    1. Pour the filling over the cooled crust.

2. Bake for 50-60 minutes, or until the center is set and the edges are lightly golden.
3. Turn off the oven and let the cheesecake cool in the oven with the door slightly open for 1 hour.
4. Refrigerate for at least 4 hours or overnight.

4. **Serve:**
    1. Top with whipped cream and garnish with lime zest or white chocolate shavings.

Lime and Pineapple Salsa

Ingredients:

- 2 cups fresh pineapple, diced
- 1 red bell pepper, diced
- ¼ cup red onion, finely chopped
- 1 jalapeño, seeded and minced (optional)
- 2 tbsp lime juice (freshly squeezed)
- ¼ cup fresh cilantro, chopped
- Salt and pepper to taste

Instructions:

1. **Combine the Ingredients:**
    1. In a bowl, mix together pineapple, red bell pepper, red onion, jalapeño (if using), lime juice, and cilantro.
2. **Season and Serve:**
    1. Season with salt and pepper to taste.
    2. Serve with grilled meats, fish, or as a dip with tortilla chips.

Lime-Honey Dressing

Ingredients:

- ¼ cup lime juice (freshly squeezed)
- 2 tbsp honey
- ¼ cup olive oil
- 1 tbsp Dijon mustard
- 1 clove garlic, minced
- Salt and pepper to taste

Instructions:

1. **Prepare the Dressing:**
    1. In a small bowl or jar, whisk together lime juice, honey, olive oil, Dijon mustard, and minced garlic.
2. **Season:**
    1. Season with salt and pepper to taste.
3. **Serve:**
    1. Drizzle over salads or use as a marinade for chicken or fish. Store any leftovers in the refrigerator for up to a week.

Lime-Infused Chicken Wings

Ingredients:

- 2 lbs chicken wings
- ¼ cup lime juice (freshly squeezed)
- 3 tbsp olive oil
- 2 cloves garlic, minced
- 1 tsp ground cumin
- 1 tsp paprika
- ½ tsp chili powder
- ¼ tsp cayenne pepper (optional)
- Salt and pepper to taste
- Lime wedges and fresh cilantro for garnish

Instructions:

1. **Marinate the Wings:**
    1. In a large bowl, mix lime juice, olive oil, minced garlic, ground cumin, paprika, chili powder, cayenne pepper (if using), salt, and pepper.
    2. Add the chicken wings and toss to coat. Marinate for at least 30 minutes, or up to overnight for more flavor.
2. **Cook the Wings:**
    1. Preheat your grill to medium-high heat or oven to 400°F (200°C).
    2. For grilling: Arrange the wings on the grill and cook for 20-25 minutes, turning occasionally, until crispy and cooked through.
    3. For baking: Place wings on a baking sheet and bake for 35-40 minutes, turning once, until crispy and cooked through.
3. **Serve:**
    1. Garnish with lime wedges and fresh cilantro before serving.

Lime and Cilantro Beef Tacos

Ingredients:

- 1 lb ground beef
- 1 tbsp olive oil
- 1 onion, finely chopped
- 2 cloves garlic, minced
- 1 tbsp ground cumin
- 1 tsp chili powder
- ½ tsp paprika
- ¼ cup lime juice (freshly squeezed)
- ¼ cup fresh cilantro, chopped
- Salt and pepper to taste
- 8 small tortillas
- Toppings: shredded lettuce, diced tomatoes, avocado slices, lime wedges

Instructions:

1. **Cook the Beef:**
    1. Heat olive oil in a large skillet over medium heat.
    2. Add onion and cook until softened, about 5 minutes.
    3. Stir in garlic, cumin, chili powder, and paprika, and cook for another minute.
    4. Add ground beef, breaking it up with a spoon, and cook until browned and fully cooked. Drain excess fat.
2. **Season the Beef:**
    1. Stir in lime juice and chopped cilantro. Season with salt and pepper to taste.
3. **Assemble the Tacos:**
    1. Warm tortillas in a dry skillet or microwave.
    2. Fill each tortilla with the beef mixture and top with shredded lettuce, diced tomatoes, avocado slices, and a squeeze of lime juice.

Lime and Jalapeño Marinade

Ingredients:

- ¼ cup lime juice (freshly squeezed)
- ¼ cup olive oil
- 2 tbsp soy sauce
- 1 tbsp honey
- 1-2 jalapeños, seeded and minced (adjust to heat preference)
- 3 cloves garlic, minced
- 1 tsp ground cumin
- 1 tsp dried oregano
- Salt and pepper to taste

Instructions:

1. **Prepare the Marinade:**
    1. In a bowl, whisk together lime juice, olive oil, soy sauce, honey, minced jalapeños, garlic, ground cumin, dried oregano, salt, and pepper.
2. **Marinate:**
    1. Use the marinade to marinate chicken, beef, pork, or tofu for at least 30 minutes, or up to 4 hours for more flavor.

Lime and Coconut Chicken Curry

Ingredients:

- 1 lb chicken breasts or thighs, cut into bite-sized pieces
- 2 tbsp coconut oil
- 1 onion, finely chopped
- 2 cloves garlic, minced
- 1 tbsp ginger, grated
- 2 tbsp curry powder
- 1 can (14 oz) coconut milk
- ¼ cup lime juice (freshly squeezed)
- 1 tbsp fish sauce (optional)
- 1 cup baby spinach or chopped cilantro
- Salt and pepper to taste
- Cooked rice for serving

Instructions:

1. **Cook the Chicken:**
    1. Heat coconut oil in a large skillet over medium heat.
    2. Add onion and cook until translucent, about 5 minutes.
    3. Stir in garlic and ginger, and cook for another minute.
2. **Add the Curry and Chicken:**
    1. Add curry powder and cook for 1 minute until fragrant.
    2. Add chicken pieces and cook until they are no longer pink.
3. **Simmer the Curry:**
    1. Stir in coconut milk, lime juice, and fish sauce (if using). Bring to a simmer and cook for 15-20 minutes, or until the chicken is fully cooked and the sauce has thickened.
4. **Finish and Serve:**
    1. Stir in baby spinach or chopped cilantro and season with salt and pepper to taste.
    2. Serve over cooked rice.

Lime-Pineapple Sorbet

Ingredients:

- 2 cups fresh pineapple, diced
- ¼ cup lime juice (freshly squeezed)
- ¼ cup honey or agave syrup
- 1 cup water
- Fresh mint leaves for garnish (optional)

Instructions:

1. **Blend the Ingredients:**
    1. In a blender, combine pineapple, lime juice, honey, and water. Blend until smooth.
2. **Freeze the Sorbet:**
    1. Pour the mixture into a shallow dish and freeze for about 2 hours, stirring every 30 minutes until the mixture is frozen and fluffy.
3. **Serve:**
    1. Scoop into bowls or glasses and garnish with fresh mint leaves if desired.

Lime-Ginger Dressing

Ingredients:

- ¼ cup lime juice (freshly squeezed)
- 2 tbsp soy sauce
- 2 tbsp honey or maple syrup
- 1 tbsp grated fresh ginger
- 2 tbsp olive oil
- 1 clove garlic, minced
- Salt and pepper to taste

Instructions:

1. **Combine Ingredients:**
    1. In a small bowl or jar, whisk together lime juice, soy sauce, honey, grated ginger, olive oil, and minced garlic.
2. **Season:**
    1. Season with salt and pepper to taste.
3. **Serve:**
    1. Drizzle over salads, grilled vegetables, or use as a marinade for meats. Store in the refrigerator for up to a week.

Lime and Cilantro Soup

Ingredients:

- 2 tbsp olive oil
- 1 onion, chopped
- 2 cloves garlic, minced
- 1 tbsp fresh ginger, grated
- 1 tsp ground cumin
- 4 cups chicken or vegetable broth
- 1 can (14.5 oz) diced tomatoes
- 1 cup corn kernels (fresh, frozen, or canned)
- 1 cup cooked chicken, shredded (optional)
- ¼ cup lime juice (freshly squeezed)
- ¼ cup fresh cilantro, chopped
- Salt and pepper to taste
- Lime wedges and additional cilantro for garnish

Instructions:

1. **Sauté the Aromatics:**
    1. Heat olive oil in a large pot over medium heat.
    2. Add onion and cook until softened, about 5 minutes.
    3. Stir in garlic and ginger, cooking for another minute.
2. **Add Broth and Tomatoes:**
    1. Stir in ground cumin, then add broth and diced tomatoes.
    2. Bring to a boil, then reduce heat and simmer for 10 minutes.
3. **Add Corn and Chicken:**
    1. Add corn and cooked chicken (if using) and cook for another 5 minutes until heated through.
4. **Finish and Serve:**
    1. Stir in lime juice and chopped cilantro. Season with salt and pepper to taste.
    2. Serve hot with lime wedges and additional cilantro for garnish.

Lime and Banana Bread

Ingredients:

- 1 ½ cups all-purpose flour
- 1 tsp baking powder
- ½ tsp baking soda
- ¼ tsp salt
- ½ cup unsalted butter, softened
- 1 cup granulated sugar
- 2 large eggs
- 1 cup mashed ripe bananas (about 3 bananas)
- ¼ cup lime juice (freshly squeezed)
- Zest of 2 limes
- 1 tsp vanilla extract

Instructions:

1. **Prepare the Oven and Pan:**
    1. Preheat your oven to 350°F (175°C) and grease a 9x5-inch loaf pan.
2. **Mix Dry Ingredients:**
    1. In a bowl, whisk together flour, baking powder, baking soda, and salt.
3. **Cream Butter and Sugar:**
    1. In a large bowl, beat butter and sugar until light and fluffy.
    2. Add eggs one at a time, beating well after each addition.
4. **Add Bananas and Lime:**
    1. Mix in mashed bananas, lime juice, lime zest, and vanilla extract.
5. **Combine and Bake:**
    1. Gradually add the dry ingredients to the wet ingredients, mixing until just combined.
    2. Pour batter into the prepared loaf pan and smooth the top.
    3. Bake for 60-70 minutes, or until a toothpick inserted into the center comes out clean.
6. **Cool and Serve:**
    1. Let the bread cool in the pan for 10 minutes before transferring to a wire rack to cool completely.

Lime-Peppercorn Pork Chops

Ingredients:

- 4 bone-in pork chops
- 2 tbsp olive oil
- 2 tbsp lime juice (freshly squeezed)
- 1 tsp black peppercorns, crushed
- 1 tsp dried thyme
- 1 tsp garlic powder
- ½ tsp onion powder
- Salt to taste

Instructions:

1. **Prepare the Pork Chops:**
    1. In a small bowl, combine lime juice, crushed peppercorns, dried thyme, garlic powder, onion powder, and salt.
    2. Rub the mixture over both sides of the pork chops.
2. **Cook the Pork Chops:**
    1. Heat olive oil in a large skillet over medium-high heat.
    2. Add pork chops and cook for 4-5 minutes per side, or until they reach an internal temperature of 145°F (63°C).
3. **Serve:**
    1. Let the pork chops rest for 5 minutes before serving.

Lime-Lavender Muffins

Ingredients:

- 1 ½ cups all-purpose flour
- 1 cup granulated sugar
- 2 tsp baking powder
- ½ tsp baking soda
- ¼ tsp salt
- ½ cup unsalted butter, melted
- 1 large egg
- 1 cup buttermilk
- ¼ cup lime juice (freshly squeezed)
- Zest of 2 limes
- 1 tbsp dried lavender flowers (culinary grade)

Instructions:

1. **Prepare the Oven and Pan:**
    1. Preheat your oven to 350°F (175°C) and line a muffin tin with paper liners.
2. **Mix Dry Ingredients:**
    1. In a bowl, whisk together flour, sugar, baking powder, baking soda, and salt.
3. **Combine Wet Ingredients:**
    1. In another bowl, whisk together melted butter, egg, buttermilk, lime juice, and lime zest.
4. **Combine and Fold:**
    1. Gradually add the wet ingredients to the dry ingredients, mixing until just combined.
    2. Gently fold in dried lavender flowers.
5. **Bake:**
    1. Divide the batter evenly among the muffin cups.
    2. Bake for 18-22 minutes, or until a toothpick inserted into the center comes out clean.
6. **Cool and Serve:**
    1. Allow muffins to cool in the tin for 5 minutes before transferring to a wire rack to cool completely.

Lime and Chipotle Salsa

Ingredients:

- 3 ripe tomatoes, diced
- 1 red onion, finely chopped
- 1 jalapeño, seeded and minced
- 2 tbsp lime juice (freshly squeezed)
- 1 tbsp chipotle peppers in adobo sauce, minced
- ¼ cup fresh cilantro, chopped
- Salt and pepper to taste

Instructions:

1. **Combine Ingredients:**
    1. In a bowl, mix together tomatoes, red onion, jalapeño, lime juice, chipotle peppers, and cilantro.
2. **Season:**
    1. Season with salt and pepper to taste.
3. **Serve:**
    1. Serve with tortilla chips, tacos, or as a topping for grilled meats.

Lime-Mango Chutney

Ingredients:

- 2 cups ripe mango, peeled and diced
- 1 onion, finely chopped
- 1 red bell pepper, diced
- 2 cloves garlic, minced
- 1 tbsp fresh ginger, grated
- ¼ cup lime juice (freshly squeezed)
- ¼ cup brown sugar
- ½ cup apple cider vinegar
- 1 tsp ground cumin
- ½ tsp ground turmeric
- ½ tsp chili flakes (adjust to taste)
- Salt to taste

Instructions:

1. **Sauté Aromatics:**
    1. In a large saucepan, heat a bit of oil over medium heat.
    2. Add onion and cook until softened, about 5 minutes.
    3. Stir in garlic and ginger, cooking for another minute.
2. **Cook the Chutney:**
    1. Add diced mango, red bell pepper, lime juice, brown sugar, apple cider vinegar, ground cumin, ground turmeric, and chili flakes to the pan.
    2. Bring to a simmer, then reduce heat and cook for 20-25 minutes, stirring occasionally, until the mango is soft and the mixture has thickened.
3. **Season and Serve:**
    1. Season with salt to taste.
    2. Allow to cool before serving. Store in an airtight container in the refrigerator for up to 2 weeks.

Lime and Coconut Smoothie

Ingredients:

- 1 cup coconut milk (canned or carton)
- 1 cup fresh pineapple chunks
- 1 ripe banana
- ¼ cup lime juice (freshly squeezed)
- 1 tbsp honey or maple syrup (optional)
- 1 cup ice

Instructions:

1. **Blend the Ingredients:**
    1. In a blender, combine coconut milk, pineapple chunks, banana, lime juice, and honey or maple syrup (if using).
    2. Blend until smooth.
2. **Add Ice:**
    1. Add ice and blend again until the mixture is chilled and frothy.
3. **Serve:**
    1. Pour into glasses and serve immediately.

Lime-Glazed Donuts

Ingredients:

- **For the Donuts:**
    - 1 ½ cups all-purpose flour
    - ½ cup granulated sugar
    - 2 tsp baking powder
    - ¼ tsp salt
    - ¼ cup unsalted butter, melted
    - 2 large eggs
    - ½ cup milk
    - 2 tbsp lime zest
- **For the Glaze:**
    - 1 cup powdered sugar
    - 2 tbsp lime juice (freshly squeezed)
    - 1 tbsp milk (if needed for consistency)

Instructions:

1. **Prepare the Donuts:**
    1. Preheat your oven to 375°F (190°C) and grease a donut pan.
    2. In a large bowl, whisk together flour, sugar, baking powder, and salt.
    3. In another bowl, combine melted butter, eggs, milk, and lime zest.
    4. Stir the wet ingredients into the dry ingredients until just combined.
2. **Bake the Donuts:**
    1. Spoon the batter into the prepared donut pan, filling each mold about ¾ full.
    2. Bake for 10-12 minutes, or until a toothpick inserted into the center comes out clean.
    3. Let cool in the pan for 5 minutes, then transfer to a wire rack to cool completely.
3. **Glaze the Donuts:**
    1. In a small bowl, whisk together powdered sugar, lime juice, and milk (if needed).
    2. Dip each donut into the glaze, allowing excess to drip off.
4. **Serve:**
    1. Allow the glaze to set before serving.

Lime and Blackberry Crumble

Ingredients:

- **For the Filling:**
    - 4 cups fresh blackberries
    - ¼ cup granulated sugar
    - 2 tbsp lime juice (freshly squeezed)
    - 1 tbsp cornstarch
    - 1 tsp lime zest
- **For the Crumble Topping:**
    - ½ cup all-purpose flour
    - ½ cup old-fashioned oats
    - ⅓ cup brown sugar
    - ¼ cup unsalted butter, cold and cut into small pieces
    - ¼ tsp salt

Instructions:

1. **Prepare the Filling:**
    1. Preheat your oven to 375°F (190°C).
    2. In a large bowl, gently toss blackberries with granulated sugar, lime juice, cornstarch, and lime zest.
    3. Transfer the blackberry mixture to a baking dish.
2. **Make the Crumble Topping:**
    1. In a separate bowl, combine flour, oats, brown sugar, and salt.
    2. Cut in cold butter with a pastry cutter or your fingers until the mixture resembles coarse crumbs.
3. **Assemble and Bake:**
    1. Sprinkle the crumble topping evenly over the blackberry mixture.
    2. Bake for 35-40 minutes, or until the topping is golden brown and the filling is bubbly.
4. **Serve:**
    1. Let cool slightly before serving. Enjoy warm with a scoop of vanilla ice cream or a dollop of whipped cream.

Lime-Coconut Energy Bars

Ingredients:

- 1 ½ cups rolled oats
- 1 cup unsweetened shredded coconut
- ½ cup almond butter or peanut butter
- ¼ cup honey or maple syrup
- ¼ cup lime juice (freshly squeezed)
- 2 tbsp lime zest
- ¼ cup chopped nuts (such as almonds or cashews)
- ¼ cup dried fruit (such as cranberries or apricots)
- Pinch of salt

Instructions:

1. **Prepare the Mixture:**
    1. In a large bowl, combine rolled oats and shredded coconut.
    2. In a microwave-safe bowl or on the stovetop, heat almond butter and honey (or maple syrup) until melted and smooth. Stir in lime juice and lime zest.
2. **Combine and Mix:**
    1. Pour the wet mixture over the oats and coconut. Add chopped nuts and dried fruit.
    2. Mix everything together until well combined. The mixture should be slightly sticky.
3. **Press and Chill:**
    1. Line an 8x8-inch baking dish with parchment paper. Press the mixture evenly into the dish.
    2. Refrigerate for at least 1-2 hours or until firm.
4. **Cut and Serve:**
    1. Lift the bars out of the dish using the parchment paper and cut into squares.
    2. Store in an airtight container in the refrigerator for up to 2 weeks.

Lime and Tequila Chicken

Ingredients:

- 4 boneless, skinless chicken breasts
- ¼ cup lime juice (freshly squeezed)
- 2 tbsp tequila
- 2 tbsp olive oil
- 3 cloves garlic, minced
- 1 tsp ground cumin
- 1 tsp paprika
- ½ tsp dried oregano
- Salt and pepper to taste
- Fresh cilantro for garnish

Instructions:

1. **Marinate the Chicken:**
    1. In a bowl, whisk together lime juice, tequila, olive oil, garlic, ground cumin, paprika, oregano, salt, and pepper.
    2. Place chicken breasts in a resealable plastic bag or shallow dish and pour marinade over them. Seal or cover and refrigerate for at least 30 minutes, or up to 4 hours.
2. **Cook the Chicken:**
    1. Preheat your grill or skillet over medium-high heat.
    2. Remove chicken from the marinade and discard the marinade.
    3. Grill or cook chicken for 6-8 minutes per side, or until the internal temperature reaches 165°F (74°C).
3. **Serve:**
    1. Let the chicken rest for a few minutes before slicing.
    2. Garnish with fresh cilantro and serve with lime wedges.

Lime and Cilantro Cornbread

Ingredients:

- 1 cup cornmeal
- 1 cup all-purpose flour
- ¼ cup granulated sugar
- 1 tbsp baking powder
- ½ tsp salt
- 1 cup buttermilk
- 2 large eggs
- ¼ cup unsalted butter, melted
- ¼ cup lime juice (freshly squeezed)
- 2 tbsp lime zest
- ¼ cup fresh cilantro, chopped

Instructions:

1. **Preheat the Oven:**
    1. Preheat your oven to 400°F (200°C) and grease an 8x8-inch baking dish or cast-iron skillet.
2. **Mix Dry Ingredients:**
    1. In a large bowl, whisk together cornmeal, flour, sugar, baking powder, and salt.
3. **Combine Wet Ingredients:**
    1. In another bowl, whisk together buttermilk, eggs, melted butter, lime juice, and lime zest.
4. **Combine and Fold:**
    1. Add wet ingredients to the dry ingredients and mix until just combined.
    2. Fold in chopped cilantro.
5. **Bake:**
    1. Pour the batter into the prepared baking dish or skillet.
    2. Bake for 20-25 minutes, or until a toothpick inserted into the center comes out clean and the top is golden brown.
6. **Cool and Serve:**
    1. Allow cornbread to cool slightly before cutting into squares.
    2. Serve warm or at room temperature.

www.ingramcontent.com/pod-product-compliance
Lightning Source LLC
LaVergne TN
LVHW081322060526
838201LV00055B/2401